THE EXTRAORDINARY LIFE OF

MICHELLE
OBAMA

D1339837

PUFFIN BOOKS

UK | USA | Canada | Ireland | Australia
India | New Zealand | South Africa

Puffin Books is part of the Penguin Random House group of companies
whose addresses can be found at global.penguinrandomhouse.com.

Coventry City
Council

STO

3 8002 02402 734 6	
Askews & Holts	Nov-2018
J973.932092 OBA JUNIO	£6.99

First published 2019

001

Text copyright © Dr Sheila Kanani, 2019
Illustrations copyright © Sarah Walsh, 2019

The moral right of the author and illustrator has been asserted

Text design by Janene Spencer
Printed and bound by CPI Group (UK) Ltd, Croydon, CR0 4YY

A CIP catalogue record for this book is available from the British Library

ISBN: 978–0–241–37273–9

All correspondence to:
Puffin Books, Penguin Random House Children's
80 Strand, London WC2R 0RL

MIX
Paper from
responsible sources
FSC® C018179

Penguin Random House is committed to a
sustainable future for our business, our readers
and our planet. This book is made from Forest
Stewardship Council® certified paper.

THE EXTRAORDINARY LIFE OF
MICHELLE OBAMA

Written by Dr Sheila Kanani
Illustrated by Sarah Walsh

EXTRAORDINARY LIVES
PUFFIN

Chicago

Chicago
Where Michelle
was born

WISCONSIN
MICHIGAN
CHICAGO
IOWA
OHIO
ILLINOIS
INDIANA
MISSOURI
KENTUCKY

WHO IS
Michelle
Obama?

Michelle LaVaughn Robinson

was born in the South Side of Chicago,

Illinois, USA, on 17 January 1964.

Michelle's parents, Fraser Robinson and Marian Shields, were normal people, with normal jobs. Her dad operated pumps for the city's water plant and her mum was a secretary for a clothing company.

Growing up, Michelle shared the living room of her family's one-bedroom apartment with her older brother, Craig. Their room was split in half by a sheet hung from the ceiling so that the two children could have a room each. Craig and Michelle were so close that people thought they were twins, even though he was nearly two years older than her.

Michelle's family didn't have a lot of money so the one-bedroom, one-bathroom apartment had to be big enough for the four of them, but they definitely still enjoyed **treats** like pizza on a Friday night, while evenings and weekends were taken up with playing board games, reading books and seeing family.

By 2016 Michelle was a lawyer, a mother of two, a writer, the founder of a charity tackling childhood obesity, a role model, an ADVOCATE for poverty awareness, a fashion icon and the first African-American First Lady of the United States of America.

> ADVOCATE: a person who publicly supports a particular cause.

So how did this sweet, smart, board-game-playing, TV-watching, pizza-loving little sister from the South Side of Chicago become one of the most *important* women in modern history?

'I wake up in a house that was BUILT BY SLAVES. I watch my daughters – TWO BEAUTIFUL, BLACK YOUNG WOMEN – head off to school, waving goodbye to their father, THE PRESIDENT OF THE UNITED STATES, the son of a man from Kenya WHO CAME HERE TO AMERICA

TO GET AN EDUCATION
*and improve his
prospects in life.'*

*I*n 1850 there lived a little girl called **Melvinia** in South Carolina. Melvinia was six years old – and she belonged to a man called David Patterson. Melvinia was a slave, and she was expected to work on the farms and do everything that she was told.

Melvinia
was illiterate –
SHE DIDN'T KNOW
HOW TO READ OR WRITE.

Melvinia's owner died in 1852 and she was sent hundreds of miles away, taken away from her few friends and everything she knew, to live with a new owner in *Georgia*.

In Georgia too there was plenty for Melvinia to be getting on with. There were cows to feed, sheep to look after, corn and cotton to plant and wheat to harvest. Melvinia was still only *eight years old*.

The Emancipation Proclamation *of 1863 was a law issued by* **Abraham Lincoln,** *the president at the time, which changed the status of some enslaved African Americans* ***from slave to free.***

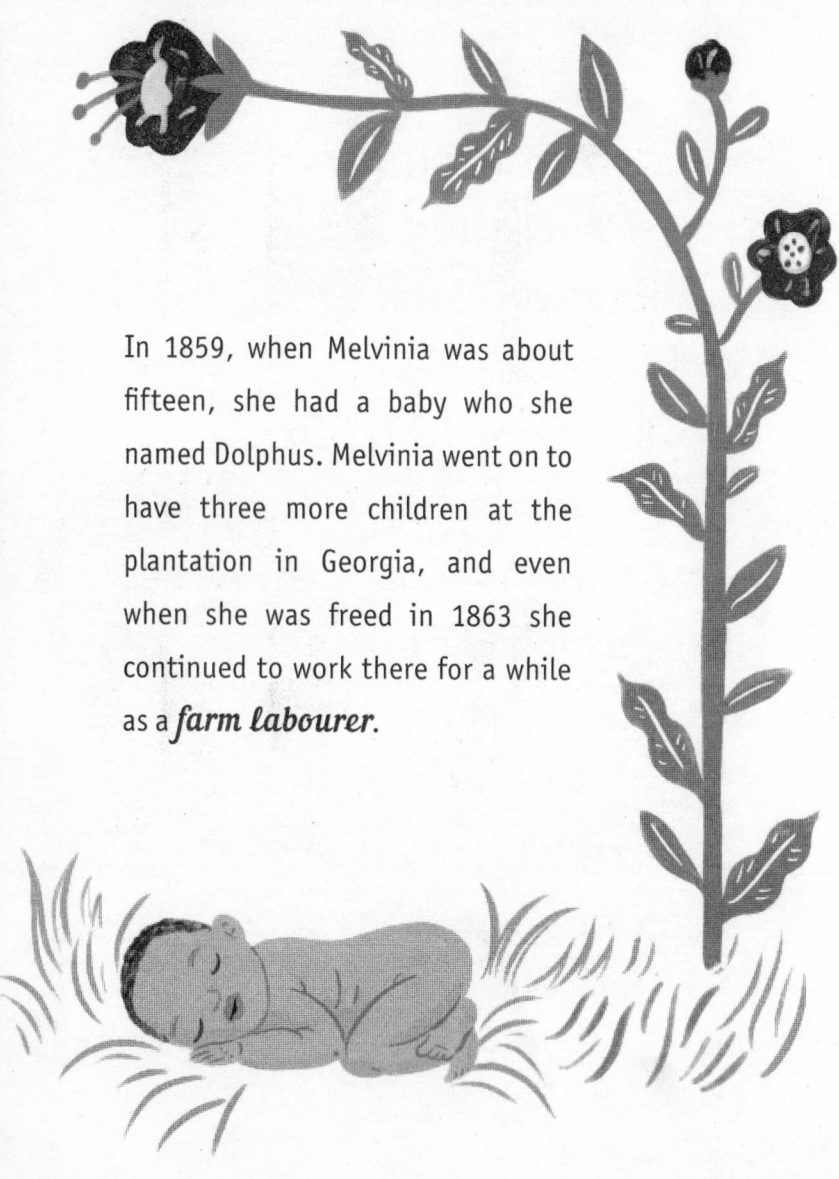

In 1859, when Melvinia was about fifteen, she had a baby who she named Dolphus. Melvinia went on to have three more children at the plantation in Georgia, and even when she was freed in 1863 she continued to work there for a while as a *farm labourer*.

DID YOU KNOW?
Michelle's middle name is LaVaughn, after her grandmother, LaVaughn Johnson.

This wasn't an unusual story for a **slave girl** in America in the 1800s. But Melvinia's great-great-great-granddaughter was Michelle LaVaughn Robinson, who has led a **remarkable** life indeed.

Michelle's early life

Michelle's early life was happy, simple and focused on **education**. Her mum stayed at home to look after the house and the children, and her dad went off to work every day. Fraser, Michelle's dad, had a condition called multiple sclerosis, which affects the brain and the spinal cord. People with multiple sclerosis can have problems with vision, balance and moving their arms and legs. But, even though he had this illness, Fraser went to work *every day* without fail. This taught Michelle the importance of working hard and never giving up.

'EVERYTHING
that I think about and do is
SHAPED AROUND
THE LIFE THAT I LIVED
in that little apartment
in the bungalow
MY FATHER WORKED
SO HARD
to provide for us.'

15

Michelle knew that the best thing she could do for her father was to take care of her studies, look after herself, and make him proud.

DID YOU KNOW?
Michelle's nickname is 'Miche' (pronounced 'Meesh').

'Seeing my father
IN PAIN,
seeing him
STRUGGLE,
watching that
every day,
IT BROKE MY HEART.'

As a family the Robinsons would watch *The Brady Bunch*, a comedy programme about a large American family in the 1970s, which was Michelle's *favourite TV show*. Michelle did chores on a Saturday, like cleaning the bathroom or mopping the floor, and on a Sunday the family would go to church and go on long drives. They always had meals together, and Michelle remembers the summers as long and fun, when the family spent time together in a cabin in White Cloud, Michigan.

'*I was surrounded by*

EXTRAORDINARY
WOMEN

*in my life who
taught me about*

QUIET STRENGTH
AND DIGNITY.'

DID YOU KNOW?

Michelle loved playing the piano so much that as a child she was often told to stop.

Michelle was fortunate to have parents who understood how important education was for their children. Her parents' **home tutoring** gave Michelle a strong start in life – both Michelle and Craig learned how to read by the age of four! The children were expected to study and get good grades; they always did chores at home and were only allowed a maximum of one hour of TV per day. Their mum Marian had once dreamed of being a PAEDIATRICIAN but never started her college education, so this could have been part of the reason she was so intent on making sure her children were ***properly educated***.

PAEDIATRICIAN: a children's doctor.

Her Great Aunt Robbie, who lived downstairs, also had a *profound effect* on Michelle. She taught Michelle the piano and singing. Great Aunt Robbie had a big bold personality, which could have influenced Michelle's approach in her fight for equality.

DID YOU KNOW?

Michelle's Great Aunt Robbie Shields was refused a place in a Northwestern University dormitory because of the colour of her skin. She sued the university – and won!

$\mathcal{M}$ichelle went to Bryn Mawr Elementary School in Chicago. By the time she was eleven years old she was on a programme for *gifted and talented students*, where she learned French and biology. When she went to high school she joined America's first state-funded 'magnet' school, Whitney M. Young Magnet High School, which had *special courses* designed to attract certain students like a magnet.

Whitney M. Young High School is open to all Chicago students, but entrance is based on good grades and entrance exam performance. Michelle was admitted because she was a *brilliant student*, but it did mean that she had to travel for over two hours every day in order to attend.

'For me, EDUCATION was power.'

Whitney M. Young High School
was named after Whitney M. Young,
a civil rights leader whose work involved
breaking down barriers of inequality and
segregation for African Americans.

'You too can realize
your dreams,
AND THEN YOUR JOB
IS TO REACH BACK
and to help someone
JUST LIKE YOU
do the same thing.'

Whitney Young is often in the top ten schools in the state of Illinois and it gives young people from disadvantaged backgrounds a *stronger chance* of succeeding in education.

Michelle thrived there. Alongside her academic work, she joined various teams and took *advanced classes*. She was a member of the National Honor Society (an ELITE group of school students) and she was the treasurer for the student council (which meant she had to watch over the finances of the committee).

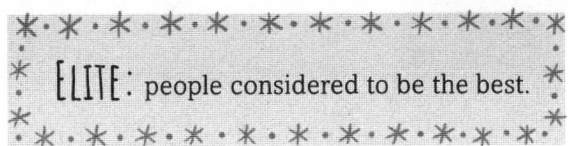

ELITE: people considered to be the best.

MICHELLE WAS GOOD AT SPORTS TOO,

but her brother said that she was very competitive and hated losing!

Despite all her **successes**, Michelle admits that she was an anxious youngster.

'I WOULD LOVE TO GO
BACK IN TIME
AND TELL MY YOUNGER SELF,
"Michelle, these middle -
and high-school years are just
a tiny blip in your life,
and all the slights and
EMBARRASSMENTS AND HEARTACHES,
all those times you got that
one question wrong on that test –
NONE OF THAT IS IMPORTANT
IN THE SCHEME OF THINGS."'

It was while at Whitney Young that Michelle first considered going to a *university* like Princeton University, an IVY LEAGUE university founded in 1746 and the fourth-oldest university in the USA. Her brother went to Princeton, and this inspired Michelle to do the same. Craig went on to become a *basketball coach* for Oregon State University and Brown University, and then for the New York Knicks basketball team.

IVY LEAGUE: a group of universities viewed as some of the best in the USA, and even in the world!

However, Michelle's path to Princeton wasn't easy. One of her school counsellors gave Michelle some **bad advice**, telling her that she should not apply to Princeton because she was setting her sights too high. But this didn't put Michelle off at all. In fact, she **studied harder**, joined more groups, did more extracurricular activities, and tried to get better and better grades. She was determined to prove the school counsellor wrong, and Michelle was accepted into Princeton in 1981. She also graduated from her high school with the title SALUTATORIAN of her class.

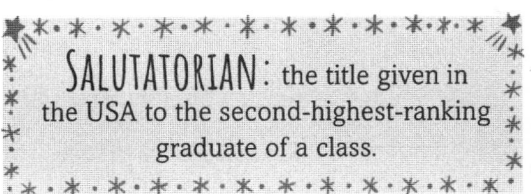

SALUTATORIAN: the title given in the USA to the second-highest-ranking graduate of a class.

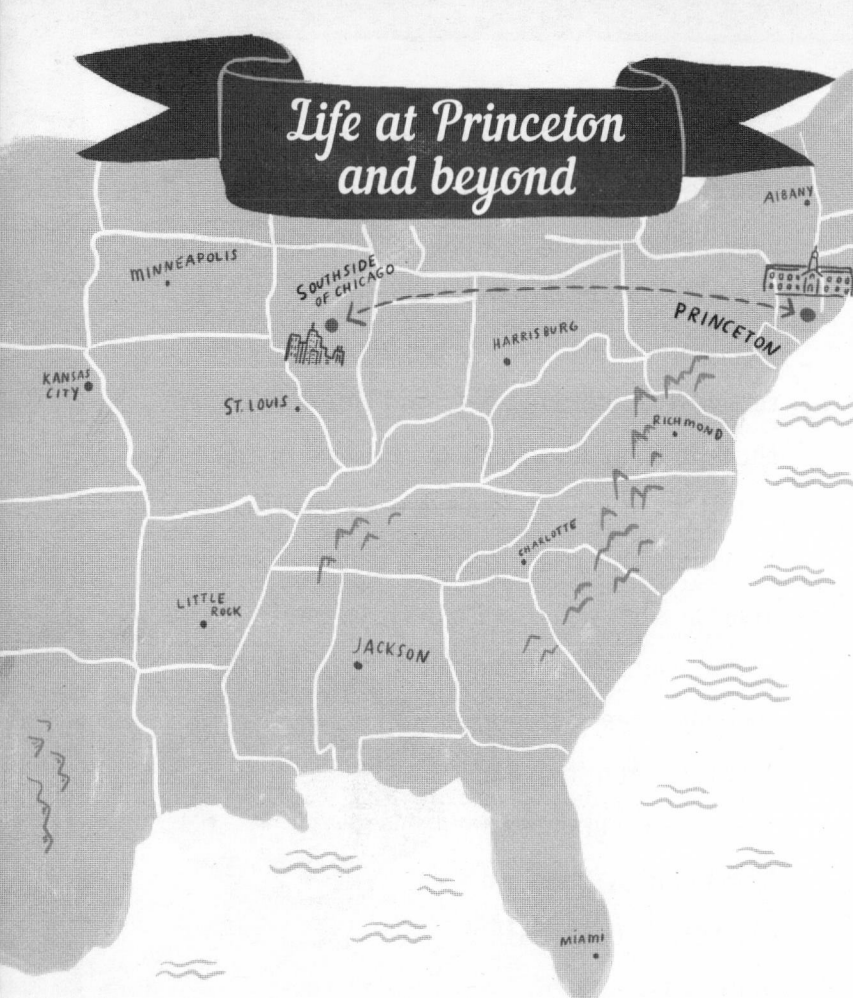

Life at Princeton and beyond

ALBANY

MINNEAPOLIS

SOUTHSIDE OF CHICAGO

HARRISBURG

PRINCETON

KANSAS CITY

ST. LOUIS

RICHMOND

LITTLE ROCK

CHARLOTTE

JACKSON

MIAMI

Going to a large Ivy League university was a **shock** to Michelle after her small apartment and community schools. Neither of her parents had been to university, and she had never visited a *college campus* before.

While she was at *Princeton*, Michelle studied SOCIOLOGY and African-American studies, and graduated with a Bachelor of Arts in 1985. Her grade was *cum laude*, which is Latin for 'with honour' or top of the class.

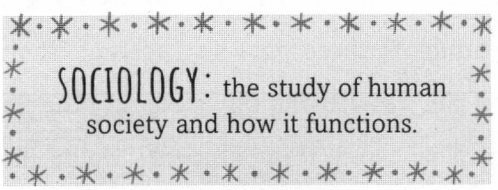

SOCIOLOGY: the study of human society and how it functions.

Unfortunately at Princeton Michelle became very aware of *racism* towards her because of the colour of her skin. She was assigned a white roommate, whose mother made her move out after one term because she didn't want her daughter sharing a room with a black girl. Michelle felt like a *fish out of water* because the other students there were so different from her – almost as if she was visiting the university the way you might visit a museum. Many students would drive to university in their BMW cars – Michelle didn't even know any adults who could afford BMWs, let alone students! But sometimes she felt that perhaps she didn't fit in with her community back home either. It was a *confusing time*.

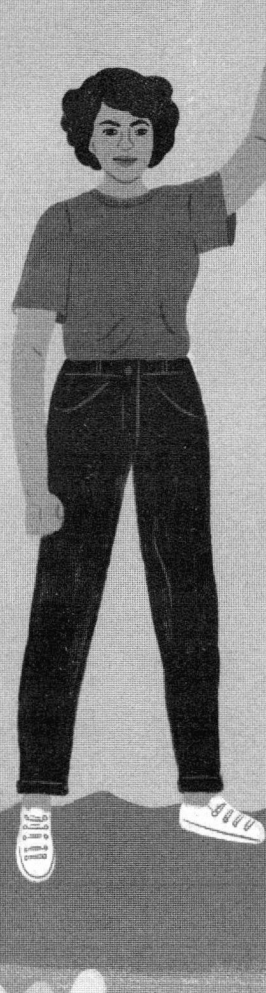

DID YOU KNOW?

The title of Michelle's final-year project (her 'thesis') was 'Princeton-Educated Blacks and the Black Community'.

But, on the whole, university life was pretty good for Michelle. Her classmates and teachers tried to understand her, and wanted her to **succeed**. Michelle also spoke up for the things she was passionate about alongside her studies. She questioned the French teaching because she thought her lessons didn't focus enough on speaking the language. She also joined the *Third World Center*, which was a group for ethnic minority students who could come together academically and culturally. In this group Michelle ran the daycare centre and did some after-school tutoring.

ETHNIC MINORITY STUDENTS
are students who are not from
a white ethnic background.

When she was collecting evidence for her thesis, Michelle interviewed black graduates from Princeton, asking them how they felt about being African American, how they felt before starting university and after, how comfortable they felt being a student, and how they felt their race had had an impact on their university life. Out of four hundred minority students at Princeton, only ninety answered her questions.

After Princeton, Michelle went to law school at **Harvard University** in Cambridge, Massachusetts. She graduated in 1988. During her time at Harvard, she campaigned for the university to hire more ethnic minority students and professors, and she helped people with low incomes find housing.

Once Michelle became a lawyer she moved back to her hometown of Chicago, where she got her *first job* at Sidley Austin law firm. It was here that her life would *change* forever.

By the time Michelle had been to Princeton and Harvard, her **confidence** in herself, her abilities and her background had grown, and she graduated with her law degree as a ***proud, well-educated, brilliant*** black woman. Her Harvard Law School professor and mentor called her *'tenacious'*, which means determined and strong-willed.

'There is
NO BOY
*who is cute
enough or
interesting
enough to stop
you from
getting your
education.'*

When Michelle met Barack

While working in marketing and INTELLECTUAL PROPERTY at Sidley Austin, Michelle was asked to *mentor* a young man from a different law firm.

> **INTELLECTUAL PROPERTY**: creations such as inventions, works of art, designs, symbols and names. They can be protected under the law, for example by copyright, to make sure the creator gets recognition or money for their work.

He hadn't finished law school yet and was sent to Sidley Austin to gain *experience* working in a different company. The young man was called Barack Obama.

Michelle was fully **qualified** at twenty-five years old, and Barack was a twenty-seven-year-old law student. They were two of only a few black people who worked at Sidley Austin at the time.

Michelle had promised her mother that she would concentrate on her work, and not dating!

Their **professional relationship** started in 1989, with business meetings, lunches with clients, and community organization meetings. But then Barack asked Michelle on a date! She politely said no, because at first she didn't think it was **appropriate** to date him because she was his mentor. As time went on, though, she realized she liked him too, despite her initial thought that he had a big nose!

DID YOU KNOW?

Barack Obama had to
play basketball with
Michelle's brother
in order to be 'allowed'
to date her.

Michelle's father and brother had often told her
that you can tell a lot about a person when you
play basketball with them. So, before dating
Barack, she made him play basketball with her
brother, Craig! Barack must have passed the test,
because afterwards she agreed to go on her *first
date* with him.

On their first date they saw a film called *Do the Right Thing*, which is about racism in Brooklyn, New York. Then they went to get ice cream and shared their *first kiss* outside a shopping centre. The shopping-centre owners later put a plaque outside, commemorating the place where Michelle and Barack kissed.

Barack Obama is quoted on the plaque, saying,

'On our first date, I treated her
to the finest ice cream
Baskin-Robbins had to offer,
our dinner table doubling
as the curb. I kissed her,
and it tasted like chocolate.'

Michelle and Barack had been dating for two years when Barack successfully completed his bar exam, making him a **qualified lawyer.** To celebrate, they went out for dinner. The waiter came out with the dessert, and there was an engagement ring!

The couple got **married** in Trinity United Church of Christ in Chicago on 3 October 1992, and they danced to Stevie Wonder's 'You And I' for their first dance.

Michelle's life changes

During her time at Sidley Austin, Michelle had **grand ambitions** to change the world, but she often found that the work did not meet her expectations and dreams. Her life changed again in 1991 when her beloved father died from complications with multiple sclerosis. Soon after, Michelle also lost a friend to cancer. These losses had a **big effect** on her and she decided to leave Sidley Austin.

'If I died in four months, is this how I would have wanted to spend this time?'

Michelle moved from working in intellectual property to working in the PUBLIC SERVICES in 1991.

PUBLIC SERVICE:
jobs in places like universities, hospitals, schools, charities and the military.

DID YOU KNOW?
Michelle still has her licence to be a lawyer but she hasn't used it since 1993.

For the next ten years Michelle tried a variety of different jobs and *excelled* in them all. She was assistant to the mayor of Chicago, she set up the Chicago office of Public Allies, and she was the associate dean of student services for the University of Chicago. During this time, she also gave birth to her daughter Malia in 1998, and Natasha (who they call Sasha) in 2001.

Public Allies was created to give young adults *opportunities* to find success in the public sector. One of the available programmes in Chicago gave participants a ten-month *apprenticeship* working for charities and government – an experience they might not have got otherwise.

'I was never
HAPPIER
IN MY LIFE
than when I was
working to build
PUBLIC ALLIES.'

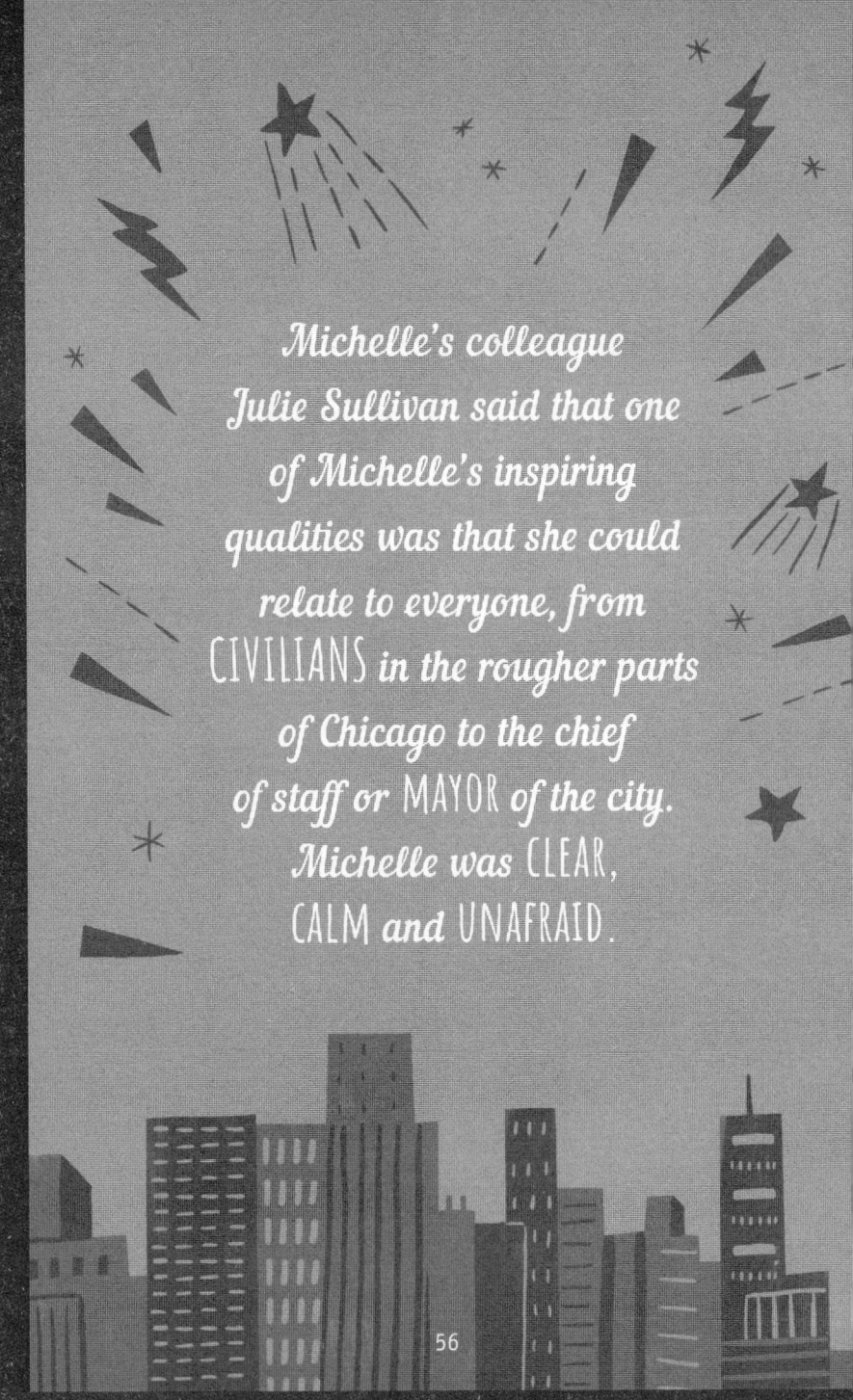

Michelle's colleague Julie Sullivan said that one of Michelle's inspiring qualities was that she could relate to everyone, from CIVILIANS in the rougher parts of Chicago to the chief of staff or MAYOR of the city. Michelle was CLEAR, CALM and UNAFRAID.

Michelle was incredibly **important** in the development of the Community Service Center in Chicago, which was set up to give students opportunities throughout the city. By this time in her career she was highly skilled and experienced in public services and she knew the community extremely well.

The road to the White House

Michelle's husband Barack was interested in a career in **politics**, and in 1996 he first joined the Illinois Senate. Michelle made sure she could continue to spend plenty of time with her young children and support her husband fully.

See the back of the book for more information about the American government.

Michelle was **supportive** of Barack's ambitions from the beginning, but she was wary about the effect of being in the public eye on her family. During early CAMPAIGNS in 2000, Michelle did everything she needed to do – she shook important people's hands, fundraised, gave interviews. But she didn't really enjoy herself. However, she did like being able to look inside other people's homes and get some tips on interior design!

CAMPAIGN: an operation planned to achieve a goal.

Barack's campaign to become a Congress representative failed, though the silver lining for Michelle was that he was able to concentrate more fully once again on their *family*.

Barack continued to pursue his dreams of a career in politics and the next big step for him was running for *senator* for the state of Illinois in 2004. This time he was successful, and this meant that he mostly worked in *Washington DC* (the capital of the USA). However, the family still lived in Chicago. Michelle decided it was best that Barack moved to Washington DC without the family, so as not to upset the day-to-day lives and education of Malia and Sasha. This meant that the girls and Michelle didn't see Barack for weeks on end, but the family always made time to talk on the phone, and Barack visited whenever he could.

At the same time, Michelle was a **working mother** climbing her own career ladder. Their young daughter Sasha was a few months old when Michelle landed herself a dream job interview at University of Chicago Hospitals.

DID YOU KNOW?

When Michelle couldn't find a babysitter for Sasha, she took her four-month-old baby with her to the job interview. Sasha slept in her car seat in the same room where her mother was being interviewed for the job!

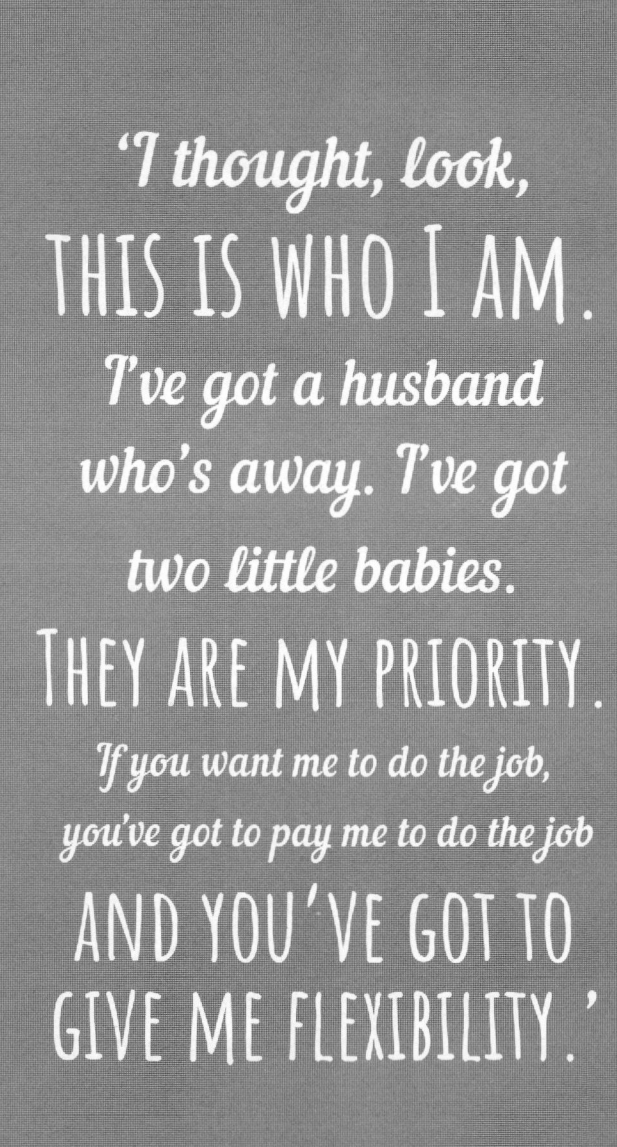

'I thought, look,
THIS IS WHO I AM.
I've got a husband
who's away. I've got
two little babies.
THEY ARE MY PRIORITY.
If you want me to do the job,
you've got to pay me to do the job
AND YOU'VE GOT TO
GIVE ME FLEXIBILITY.'

Her **honesty** about why she needed to bring her baby along to the interview was taken in the best way possible and Michelle got the job. She continued to work at the University of Chicago Hospitals for a few years after that, working her way up to **vice president.**

Michelle was called 'tenacious' once again – this time by Kenneth P. Kates, the chief operating officer at the University of Chicago Hospitals.

In 2007, when his daughters were both under ten, Barack Obama announced that he was running for *US president*. Because Barack's job meant more and more time away from Michelle, she moved to be with him in Washington DC while her mother looked after the girls.

Michelle and Barack made a deal: Michelle would fully support Barack in running for president only if he agreed to give up smoking if he won!

During this time, Michelle threw herself into the presidential campaign trail. She was often quoted in the newspaper and on TV, and many people were, at first, surprised by her **strength**, **individuality** and **honest opinions**.

'I TEASE MY HUSBAND.
He is incredibly smart,
and he is very able to deal with
A STRONG WOMAN,
which is one of the
reasons why he can be
PRESIDENT,
because he can
DEAL WITH ME.'

Michelle **spoke openly** about causes close to her heart, like family values and the position of women in society, and instead of trying to be like past wives of political figures she asked people to see her as the **individual** that she had worked hard to become. She was keen for her and Barack to continue to have separate professional relationships and work together as a **family** as well as a couple.

DID YOU KNOW?
Michelle and the children love playing jokes on Barack Obama!

During the campaign, Michelle used her new-found *platform* to discuss issues that concerned her, like family, race, motherhood and education. Early on in the campaign she tried to limit how much she did, but by 2008 she had no time for her own work: she once attended thirty-three presidential events in eight days! Michelle worked with significant figures like Oprah Winfrey, writing her own speeches and delivering them with style and confidence (and no notes!).

'When someone
is cruel or acts like
a bully, you don't
stoop to their level.
No, our motto is,

WHEN THEY GO LOW,

WE GO HIGH.'

Rising above the criticism

It was around this time that some people began to *complain* about Michelle, sometimes flinging racist or sexist taunts at her. Some people called her an 'angry black woman' and accused her of being UNPATRIOTIC, even attacking her for her honesty. Some people perhaps felt threatened by how *intelligent* she was, and how she was using her platform to fight for what she believed in.

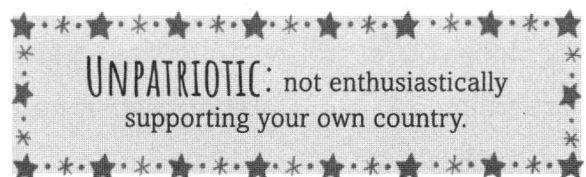

UNPATRIOTIC: not enthusiastically supporting your own country.

Sometimes the media was **unsupportive** of Michelle, but she took it all in her stride and didn't let it get her down.

Michelle's fashion sense also came under SCRUTINY. Whether she wore smart office wear or more informal clothes, someone always had a comment!

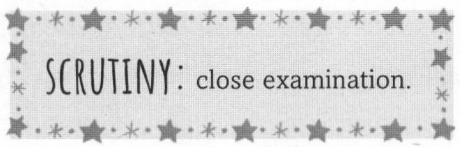

SCRUTINY: close examination.

But by the summer of 2008 the media had softened towards Michelle. She had been interviewed on popular talk shows and for magazines, but was still doing more serious *interviews* on the evening news.

'When you're out campaigning,

THERE WILL ALWAYS BE
CRITICISM.

*I just take it in stride,
and at the end of the day,
I know that it comes
with the territory.*'

FLOTUS

B arack Obama was elected as US president in November 2008 and was INAUGURATED in January 2009. This meant that in 2009 Michelle formally became the *First Lady* of the United States, or the 'FLOTUS'. This is the title held by the wife of the president of the USA. (There have been no male spouses of presidents to date.)

INAUGURATION: official introduction.

As FLOTUS, Michelle decided to impose her own *independence* on the role. Instead of learning about past First Ladies and trying to be like them, Michelle decided to define the role in her own special way. She wanted to use her *power* to address issues and causes important to her, based on who she was as an *individual*.

'I knew that I would have to find this role very

VERY UNIQUELY
and
SPECIFICALLY TO ME
and who I was.'

Michelle became more and more experienced in *political campaigns*, and in how to show herself to the media and the public. Many now believe that she is the most popular FLOTUS of all time, with people thinking of her as sensitive, sharp and deeply loyal. Michelle was *popular* partly because of how she portrayed herself and her family, reminding everyone that they also enjoyed 'normal' things like gardening and playing with their children.

DID YOU KNOW?
The family have two dogs called Sunny and Bo.

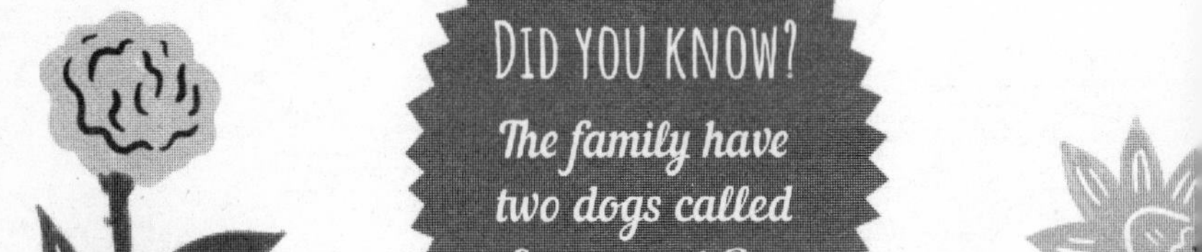

MICHELLE'S SECRET SERVICE CODE NAME IS RENAISSANCE. BARACK OBAMA'S IS RENEGADE.

Since becoming First Lady in 2009 Michelle used her position to campaign for her own causes and charities, while also becoming a *fashion icon*, and remaining strong in her role as a *mother*.

Campaigns and causes

When Michelle's husband was elected as president of the United States, she didn't just sit back and enjoy the fame and fortune. She started as she meant to go on, first by visiting homeless shelters and soup kitchens, looking out for those less fortunate than herself. She continued her public service work. The difference this time was that she did it as the *First Lady*.

Michelle supported many of Barack's policies and promoted his ideas through her own **campaigns**. She hosted receptions at the White House for women's rights, visited the US departments for housing and education, and tried to get to know the government inside and out.

Some people thought her work was notable; others thought she should be less involved in her husband's politics. Either way, she was a *force to be reckoned with!*

'I ADMIT IT:
I am louder
than the average
human being and have
NO FEAR
OF SPEAKING MY MIND.
These traits don't come
from the color of my skin
but from an unwavering
BELIEF
IN MY OWN INTELLIGENCE.'

Let's Move!

*I*n 2010 Michelle started the 'Let's Move!' initiative, trying to reduce, and hopefully reverse, the twenty-first-century trend of **childhood obesity**. Previous First Ladies had supported the use of organic foods in the White House kitchen, and Michelle took it one step further by planting the **White House Kitchen Garden** and installing beehives on the lawns. This meant that state dinners could include home-grown fruit and veg and **home-produced honey**!

Her 'Let's Move!' campaign was joined by Barack's *Task Force on Childhood Obesity*, which reviewed national INITIATIVES. She still promotes healthy eating to everyone, from her own daughters to the US Department of Defense, although she admits to enjoying French fries and desserts now and again. She reminds us that she is human too!

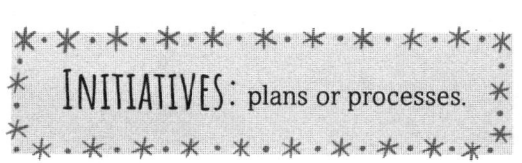

INITIATIVES: plans or processes.

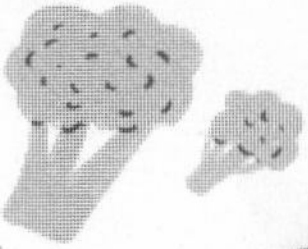

DID YOU KNOW?
Michelle made a rule that the White House kitchen could only make healthy organic food.

'*Let's Move!*' encourages healthy eating and lifestyles with better food labelling, healthier food in schools and more physical activity. Michelle hopes to reduce childhood obesity by 2030. For the campaign a song called 'Move Your Body' was released and there was a special **Flash Workout** that came with it. The song was by Beyoncé and was filmed in a real school canteen.

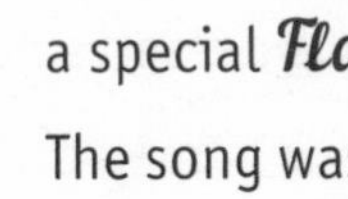

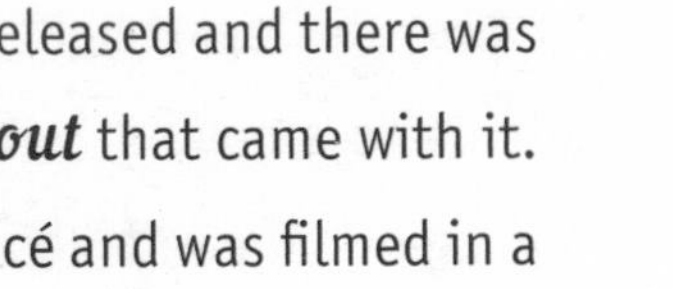

DID YOU KNOW?

The workout for 'Move Your Body' was created by the same person who choreographed Beyoncé's 'Single Ladies'!

CHOREOGRAPHY: the art of creating a dance.

Joining Forces

In 2011 Michelle worked to support VETERANS and people in the military and their families through a variety of programmes under the initiative '**Joining Forces**', which she set up with fellow educator Jill Biden.

> VETERAN: a person who has previously served in the military.

'Joining Forces' helped veterans with employment opportunities, education, mental wellbeing, and other tools they might need to have a ***successful life*** after leaving the military. Michelle hoped that this initiative would also connect the American public with the military and showcase their experience, skills and dedication.

Working with ***veterans***, in particular working women and military families, Michelle was often moved to tears when hearing stories of what they had encountered. She also encouraged openly gay and lesbian military people to work with her for 'Joining Forces'. She was publicly in favour of ***same-sex marriages***. For her work with these groups, Michelle has won a lot of praise.

'It really comes down
to the values of
FAIRNESS AND EQUALITY
we want to pass down . . .

And in a country where
we teach our children that
EVERYONE
IS EQUAL UNDER THE LAW,
discriminating
against same-sex couples
JUST ISN'T RIGHT.'

Michelle has also used *social media* in a positive way, and to back campaigns or show her support for people. She often tweets and uses hashtags. In 2014 she tweeted a picture of herself holding a poster that said *#bringbackourgirls*, which was a campaign trying to bring about the return of schoolgirls who had been kidnapped in Nigeria.

BRING BACK ♥OUR♥ GIRLS!

As ever, there were people who **criticized** Michelle for her work. No matter how much she did or didn't do, there was always someone out there who had an opinion. Some people thought she was wrong to use her position to tackle obesity rather than doing more for women's rights.

Michelle has travelled the world, and she often gives **inspirational speeches** when she visits new places. She has spoken at graduation ceremonies, political marches, sporting events and anniversary ceremonies. She has met Queen Elizabeth at Buckingham Palace, the Pope, the king of Saudi Arabia and Nelson Mandela.

DID YOU KNOW?
Although it isn't normally allowed, when Michelle met the Queen she gave her a hug!

Inspirational

Michelle has become a *style icon* as well as an inspiration for her work. Michelle has featured in articles from 'Twenty-five of the World's Most Inspiring Women' to 'Ten of the World's Best Dressed People'.

DID YOU KNOW?
Michelle hates wearing tights!

She is a positive role model for all women, but perhaps especially for African-American women, and has

DID YOU KNOW?

She rapped with Missy Elliott and James Corden in an episode of 'Carpool Karaoke'.

featured on the front cover of some high-profile fashion magazines like *Vogue*. Sometimes the media has concentrated more on what Michelle wore than her excellent work, but she has used her fame positively, and sometimes even with a *sense of humour*!

She has featured as a character in popular *cartoons*, such as *The Simpsons*, and she made an appearance on Jimmy Fallon's popular 'Ew!' sequence where she danced with actor Will Ferrell.

Reach Higher

*E*ducation has always been important to Michelle, and she was determined to use her experience to show that *everyone* can change their future and improve their education. She created the *'Reach Higher'* programme to inspire young people to take charge of their education after high school.

'You have to stay in school.

YOU HAVE TO.

You have to go to college.
You have to get your degree.

BECAUSE THE ONE THING
people can't take away
from you is

YOUR EDUCATION.

And it is worth
the investment.'

Michelle hoped that by the year 2020 America would have the most university graduates in the world!

With her fame and popularity, Michelle
helped her husband get re-elected as president
for a second term running in 2012.

A voice for young girls

*I*n 2015 Michelle and Barack Obama created the *'Let Girls Learn'* initiative. Michelle and her team noticed that girls face many challenges when it comes to education, and are working towards helping girls reach their FULL ACADEMIC POTENTIAL.

> FULL ACADEMIC POTENTIAL:
> getting everything you can out of your education.

As a young girl, Michelle was nurtured and encouraged to do well academically, and she wants *all young girls* to have that chance in life.

'I had the honor of meeting

MALALA YOUSAFZAI,

who was shot in the head
just for trying to go to school . . .
There are tens of millions
of girls like Malala
in every corner of the globe
who are not in school –
girls who are so

BRIGHT, HARD-WORKING
AND HUNGRY TO LEARN.'

In 2016 Michelle Obama and talk-show host Oprah Winfrey had an hour-long discussion about women's issues in America. Michelle encouraged women across the country to *put themselves first*.

'We need to do a
BETTER JOB
of putting ourselves
HIGHER on our own
"to do" list.'

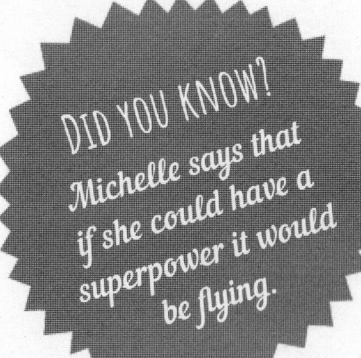

DID YOU KNOW?
Michelle says that
if she could have a
superpower it would
be flying.

Life after the White House

When Barack's second TERM as president came to an end in 2016, the race began for a **new president**. The two main candidates were Hillary Clinton and Donald Trump. Michelle made many speeches **in favour** of Hillary Clinton, but in November 2016 Donald Trump was elected as the new president of the USA.

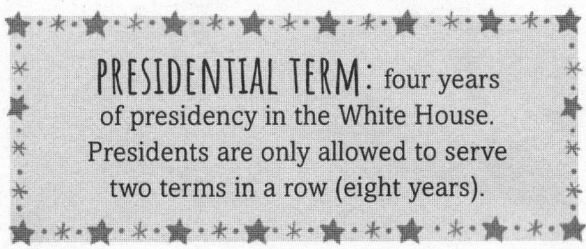

PRESIDENTIAL TERM: four years of presidency in the White House. Presidents are only allowed to serve two terms in a row (eight years).

It was the end of the Obamas' time in the White House, but it was not the end of Michelle's **ambitions** to make the world a better place.

Unlike Hillary Clinton (who was also once a First Lady), Michelle's future ambitions do not include running for president. Barack has even said, 'There are three things that are certain in life: death, taxes and Michelle is **not running for president.**'

Michelle herself has said that she plans never to run for president because she wants to have an impact in the world **without being biased**.

She would, however, like to continue to serve the public without CONTROVERSY, and she would also like to spend more time with her children. Sasha was only seven when her dad became president, so when they left the White House Michelle looked forward to the children getting to spend some time *outside the limelight*.

> CONTROVERSY: disagreement or argument, usually on a topic that affects a lot of people.

Leaving the White House wasn't too much of a disappointment for Michelle, who believed that without the constraints of being the First Lady, and without the media watching her every step, her position could be *even more powerful*. While still in that position, she had said, 'There is a potential that my voice could be heard by many people who can't hear me now because I'm Michelle Obama, the First Lady'.

She continued her campaigns for health and education, which she calls 'the single *most important civil rights* issue that we face today'. The Obamas have enjoyed travelling, visiting friends and family and spending time outside the public eye. Their daughter Malia went on to go to Harvard University, just like her mother.

Michelle Obama has accomplished so much in her time as a lawyer, a public servant and as the First Lady. Her life has been an *extraordinary* one so far – and she will continue to work hard to make life better for young people across the world.

'Young people,
don't be afraid.
BE FOCUSED, BE
DETERMINED,
BE HOPEFUL,
BE EMPOWERED . . .

Lead by example
WITH HOPE,
NEVER FEAR,
and know that
I will be with you,
ROOTING FOR YOU
and working to
support you for
the rest of my life.'

TIMELINE

17 January 1964
Michelle is born.

1977
Michelle graduates
from Bryn Mawr
Elementary
School.

1970
Michelle starts Bryn Mawr
Elementary School.

1988
Michelle graduates from Harvard Law School and joins Sidley Austin law firm.

1985
Michelle graduates from Princeton University.

1989
Michelle meets Barack Obama. They go on their first date.

1981
Michelle graduates from Whitney M. Young Magnet High School.

1992
Michelle marries
Barack Obama.

1991
Michelle's father dies.
Michelle starts working in
public services, becoming
assistant to the mayor of
Chicago. Michelle and
Barack become engaged.

1993
Michelle becomes the
founding member and
executive director for
the Chicago office of
Public Allies.

1996
Michelle is associate dean
of student services at the
University of Chicago.
She is also director of the
University Community
Service Center. Barack
joins the Illinois Senate.

1998
Michelle gives birth to her
first daughter, Malia.

2005
Michelle becomes vice president for community and external affairs at University of Chicago Hospitals.

2004
Barack becomes Illinois state senator.

2002
Michelle starts to work for University of Chicago Hospitals as the executive director for community affairs.

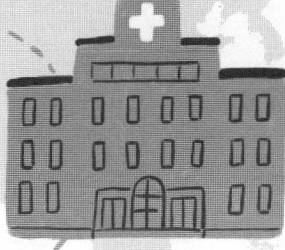

2001
Michelle gives birth to daughter Sasha.

2000
Michelle helps Barack on his campaign for senator, which he loses.

2008

Barack Obama is elected president of the United States.

2009

Michelle becomes First Lady of the United States as husband Barack officially becomes president of the United States. She features on the front cover and in a photo spread in *Vogue* magazine.

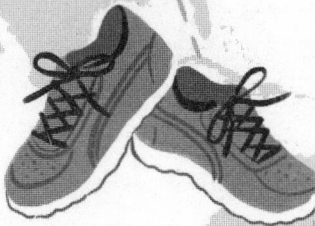

2010

Michelle starts the 'Let's Move' campaign against childhood obesity.

2011

Michelle works with Dr Jill Biden to launch the 'Joining Forces' initiative to support service people, veterans and families. Michelle meets Nelson Mandela.

2015

Michelle launches another campaign called 'Let Girls Learn', which has a global focus on girls' education.

2014

Michelle starts the 'Reach Higher' campaign.

2013

Michelle is the first First Lady to announce the winner of an Oscar.

2012

Barack Obama is elected to be the president for his second term.

2017
Michelle gives final speech as First Lady.
Michelle and Barack celebrate twenty-five years
of marriage.

2018
Michelle enjoys life after the
White House and remains an
advocate for empowering
young people.

More about the American Government

*T*he United States of America is governed by teams of people who have been elected by the public – CONGRESS – and one leader, the elected president. The USA is split into fifty states, bound together and goverened by the president. Each state has some of its own laws in addition to America's *federal* laws, which the people living in that state need to abide by.

> CONGRESS is the collection of people who have the power to make new laws, or change existing ones. They vote on the law – and if it gets a majority, it must then be signed by the president.

The president is therefore the most *important person* in the US government – and the president's spouse (in this case, Michelle Obama, the First Lady) features prominently in the politics of the country, and can be very influential!

Index

Bryn Mawr Elementary School 22

Clinton, Hillary 100, 102

Harvard Law School 36–7

Joining Forces 84–5

'Let Girls Learn' 95
'Let's Move!' 80–83
Lincoln, Abraham 11

Melvinia (Michelle's great-great-
　　great-grandmother) 8–13

Obama, Barack:
　　after the White House 104
　　and Michelle 38–47, 66, 102
　　in politics 58–60, 64
　　as president 6, 73, 81, 94
Obama, Malia 6, 52, 60, 104
Obama, Michelle
　　after the White House 100–107
　　at Harvard Law School 36–37
　　at Princeton University 28–35
　　at school 22–29
　　at Sidley Austin law firm 36, 39–40, 48
　　at University of Chicago Hospitals 61–3
　　and Barack Obama 38–47, 64–5, 66
　　birth and childhood 1–21
　　family history 8–13
　　as First Lady 4, 6–7, 73–99
　　and politics 58–60, 64–71
　　in public services 50–57
　　Timeline 108–114
Obama, Sasha 6, 52, 60, 61, 103

Princeton University 28–35
Public Allies 52, 54–5

racism 21, 32
'Reach Higher' 92–3
Robinson, Craig 2, 20, 26, 28, 43
Robinson, Fraser 2, 14–17, 48
Robinson, Marian 2, 14, 20, 64

Shields, Robbie 21
Sidley Austin 36, 39–40, 48
slavery 8–13
social media 87

Trump, Donald 100

University of Chicago Hospitals 61–3

Whitney M. Young High School 22–5, 29
Winfrey, Oprah 67, 97

Yousafzai, Malala 96

Quote Sources

Direct quotes throughout are from Michelle Obama's speeches and addresses, except the below:

Page 15: 'The Stunning Transformation of Michelle Obama' (www.thelist.com article by Lauren Bair)

Pages 19, 98: 'Michelle Obama: Even More Inspiring Than We Realised . . .' (*Marie Claire* article by Francesca Rice, 16 January 2015)

Page 23: 'Michelle Obama: This issue is personal for me' (CNN, 13 October 2016)

Page 27: 'Michelle Obama: Advice to My Younger Self' (*PEOPLE* magazine, 12 October 2014)

Page 49: 'Michelle's Life' (*New York* magazine, 15 March 2009)

Page 62: The White House Working Families Summit (23 June 2014)

Page 65: 'Michelle Obama: "I've Got a Loud Mouth"' (ABC News, 22 May 2007)

Page 71: *The Obama Presidency: A Preliminary Assessment* (edited by Douglas M. Brattebo, Robert P. Watson, Tom Lansford; 2012)

Page 75: 'The nine important things Michelle Obama and Oprah said last night' (*Washington Post* article by Krissah Thompson, 15 June 2016)

Page 79: 'A Real Wife, in a Real Marriage' (*Newsweek* article by Raina Kelley, 16 February 2008)

Page 86: 'Michelle Obama Supports Marriage Equality So That "Everyone Is Equal Under The Law"'(*ThinkProgress* article Tara Culp-Ressler, June 2012)

Look out for these other extraordinary lives!

Available now:

The *Extraordinary Life of Malala Yousafzai*

The *Extraordinary Life of Michelle Obama*

The *Extraordinary Life of Stephen Hawking*

Coming soon:

The *Extraordinary Life of Anne Frank*

The *Extraordinary Life of Neil Armstrong*

The *Extraordinary Life of Katherine Johnson*

The *Extraordinary Life of Mahatma Gandhi*

The *Extraordinary Life of Rosa Parks*

The *Extraordinary Life of Mary Seacole*